# ONE HUNDRED WAYS OF
# COOKING EGGS

BY
## FILIPPINI
(TWENTY-FIVE YEARS WITH DELMONICO)

**Creative Cookbooks**
**Monterey, California**

One Hundred Ways of Cooking Eggs

by
Alessandro Filippini

ISBN: 1-58963-679-1

Reprinted from the 1892 edition

Creative Cookbooks
An Imprint of Fredonia Books
Monterey, California
http://www.creativecookbooks.com

# A WORD OF ADVICE.

---

Eggs are not fit for any purpose unless they are PERFECTLY fresh. An easy method of ascertaining the freshness of an egg is to hold it toward the sun or toward a good light. If fresh, it will be perfectly clear; if it is clear on one side and cloudy on the other, it is stale. Another good test is to place the eggs in a pan filled with water; those that sink to the bottom are perfectly fresh; if they float at the top or stand on end in the water, they are unfit for use.

# NOTES.

A pinch of salt represents 205 grains, or a tablespoonful.

Half a pinch of pepper represents 38 grains, or a teaspoonful.

A third of a pinch of nutmeg represents 13 grains, or half a tea-spoonful.

The recipes referred to in the "One Hundred Ways of Cooking Eggs" will be found in the appendix.

# CONTENTS.

# CONTENTS.

# 1. *Poached.*

Boil in a deep saucepan three quarts of water with a heavy pinch of salt and three drops of vinegar. Have easily at hand twelve fresh eggs. When, and only when, the water boils, rapidly but carefully crack six of them, one by one. As success to have them in proper shape and cooked to perfection depends upon how they are handled, special care should be taken to crack them as rapidly as possible, carefully avoiding to break the yolks, and dropping each one right on the spot where the water bubbles, and as near the boiling-point as possible. Poach for one minute and a quarter from the time that the water boils after the eggs were put in. Lift them up with a skimmer, lay them on the freshly prepared toasts, or use for any other desired purpose; and repeat the same with the other six. If handled strictly as above described you will have them to perfection, and no necessity of trimming any superfluous adherings; serve when required.

9

## 2. Scrambled Eggs.

Melt three ounces of butter in a saucepan, break into it twelve fresh eggs; season with a pinch of salt, half a pinch of pepper, and a third of a pinch of grated nutmeg. Mix thoroughly without stopping for three minutes, using a spatula, and having the pan on a very hot stove. Turn into a warm tureen, add a little verjuice or lemon juice, and send to the table very hot.

## 3. Scrambled Eggs with Asparagus Tops.

To be prepared exactly the same as for No. 2. After the eggs have been well mixed with butter in the pan, there is added a quarter of a bunch of freshly boiled asparagus-tops.

10

## 4. *Scrambled Eggs with Truffles.*

Place in a saucepan four good-sized, sliced truffles with a glassful of Madeira wine. Reduce to about half, which will take two minutes; add a tablespoonful of butter; season with one pinch of salt and half a pinch of pepper. Crack into the saucepan twelve eggs, mix all well together with the spatula for three minutes on a very hot stove without stopping. Turn into a hot tureen and serve.

## 5. *Scrambled Eggs with Smoked Beef.*

Fry in a sautoire for one minute two ounces of finely minced smoked beef. Scramble twelve eggs as for No. 2, mixing with the above prepared beef. Any kind of garnishing may be added to the scrambled eggs.

## 6. *Scrambled Eggs with Chicory.*

Blanch for fifteen minutes a good-sized head of chicory; drain it and cut it into one-inch lengths. Put these in a saucepan on the hot stove with an ounce of butter and one minced onion, fry, and then moisten with half a pint of broth (No. 101), adding a pinch of salt and half a pinch of pepper. Let cook until all the liquid is evaporated (which will take from twenty to twenty-two minutes). Break twelve eggs into a saucepan, add the chicory and another ounce of butter, then scramble with a spatula all together for four minutes, and serve with heart-shaped bread croûtons (No. 102) around the dish.

## 7. *Eggs à la Livingston.*

Cover six pieces of cut toast with pâté-de-foie-gras, lay them on a dish, and pour twelve scrambled eggs over (No. 2), add two tablespoonfuls of demi-glace around the dish and serve (No. 103).

## 8. *Eggs à la Bourguignonne.*

Place in a saucepan one tablespoonful of meat-glaze with one pint of broth (No. 101). Boil, then crack into it two fresh eggs, and poach for one and a quarter minutes. Carefully lift up with a skimmer, and gently lay them on a hot silver dish. Repeat the same operation with ten more, two at a time; when all on the dish, sprinkle over them an ounce of grated Parmesan cheese. Place in the hot oven to brown for one minute. Reduce the gravy in which they were poached to one-half, then carefully pour the sauce around the eggs, but not over them, and serve hot.

13

## 9. *Fried Eggs.*

Place in a frying-pan on the hot range three tablespoonfuls of very good sweet oil, heat it well, then carefully break into it one fresh egg, being careful not to break the yolk, and with the aid of a table knife fold the white right over the yolk, cook for a quarter of a minute, turn it over with a cake-turner, cook for a quarter of a minute on the other side, lift it up with the cake-turner, dress on a hot dish with a folded napkin. Proceed precisely the same way with eleven more, and then they will be ready to serve for any purpose desired.

N. B.—Mix one pinch of salt, and half a pinch of white pepper, and as soon as the eggs are dressed on the dish season each one evenly with it; taking special care to cook them separately, and no more than a quarter of a minute on each side.

14

## 10. *Eggs au Beurre Noir.*

Put one ounce of butter in a frying-pan on the hot stove, let heat well, but not brown; break gently into a dish twelve very fresh eggs, slide them carefully into the pan, then season with a pinch of salt and half a pinch of white pepper; let cook slowly for three minutes. Have ready a hot, flat dish, slide the eggs gently onto it, without turning them over, and be careful to avoid breaking them; lay the dish containing the eggs in a warm place. Put two ounces of butter in the same pan, place it on the hot stove, and let the butter get a good brown color for three minutes, then drop in two teaspoonfuls of vinegar. Pour this over the eggs, and serve.

## 11. *Eggs au Soleil.*

Put two tablespoonfuls of lard in a frying-pan on the hot stove, break in twelve fresh eggs, dropping them in carefully, one by one; let them cook for two minutes, then with a skimmer take each one up separately and lay it carefully on a dry cloth. Have some fritter-batter (No. 104) ready, cut a piece of half-cooked bacon into small, square pieces of about an inch, and add them to the batter, then dip in the eggs, one after the other, taking up with each one a piece of the bacon, and with the fingers drop them into very hot grease, and cook to a good golden color for two minutes. Lift them up with the skimmer, lay them on a dry cloth to drain; sprinkle over half a pinch of salt, dress on a hot dish with a folded napkin, and serve.

## 12. *Eggs à la Béchamel.*

Pour one pint of béchamel (No. 108) into a saucepan, and put it on the hot stove. Cut twelve hard-boiled eggs in halves, add them to the hot béchamel; season with half a pinch of white pepper, and let heat thoroughly for three minutes, but be careful not to let it boil. Add one ounce of butter and a saltspoonful of grated nutmeg, then pour it on a hot serving-dish, and serve with six heart-shaped croûtons (No. 102).

### 13. *Eggs à la Pauvre Femme.*

Heat half an ounce of butter in a dish on the hot stove, then break into it twelve fresh eggs, and sprinkle over two ounces of fresh bread-crumbs. Set the dish in the hot oven, and let bake for two minutes; then pour over the eggs half a pint of well-reduced Espagnole sauce (No. 105), add three ounces of cooked, tender ham, or cooked kidneys cut up finely, and serve.

## 14.  *Eggs  au  Gratin.*

Knead well together in a bowl, one tablespoonful of bread-crumbs, two ounces of butter, three chopped anchovies, a pinch of parsley, a pinch of chervil, one chopped shallot, three raw egg yolks, a good pinch of salt, half a pinch of white pepper, and a pinch of grated nutmeg.   When ready, put these ingredients into a silver baking-dish (by preference) with one ounce of butter at the bottom.   Place it on a slow fire for two minutes, then break over it six eggs, which will be plenty; cook for five minutes in the hot oven, remove, lay the dish on top of another, and serve immediately.

## 15. *Eggs à la Tripe.*

Fry two medium-sized, sound, sliced onions in a frying-pan with two ounces of butter, but do not brown them; mix in half a spoonful of flour, and a large cupful of sweet cream; season with a pinch of salt, half a pinch of white pepper, and the third of a pinch of grated nutmeg. Cook for eight minutes, stirring constantly with the spatula; then add twelve sliced, hard-boiled eggs, and heat together thoroughly for two minutes without letting it boil again; pour on a hot dish and serve.

## 16. *Eggs à la Vanderbilt.*

Place one ounce of good butter on a silver dish, set it on the hot stove, and break in twelve fresh eggs, being careful not to disturb the yolks; season with a light pinch of salt and the third of a pinch of pepper; then let cook slowly for four minutes. Pour over the eggs a pint of hot Vanderbilt garnishing as for the omelet (No. 67), and serve immediately.

## 17. *Eggs à la Valencienne.*

Put into a saucepan half a pint of hot, boiled rice, half a pint of hot tomato sauce, two good - sized mushrooms, cut julienne-shaped, one truffle cut the same, and two tablespoonfuls of grated Parmesan cheese; season with half a pinch of salt, half a pinch of pepper, and the third of a pinch of grated nutmeg, and let cook on the hot stove for five minutes, stirring it lightly with the spatula. Leave the pan on the corner of the stove to keep warm, while putting half an ounce of good butter on a silver dish, and when placed on the hot stove, crack in twelve fresh eggs, being careful not to break the yolks; season with half a pinch of salt and the third of a pinch of pepper, then let cook for two minutes. Dress the prepared garnishing in four dome-shaped heaps—one at each end of the dish, and one at each side—and serve immediately.

## 18. *Eggs à la Provençale.*

Pour two tablespoonfuls of oil into a small frying-pan, and set it on the fire. When well heated, break one egg into a bowl, season with a pinch of salt and half a pinch of pepper (divided up for the twelve eggs), then drop it into the oil; baste the egg with a spoon, turn it over, and when a good color on both sides, drain it on a wire sieve. Cook the twelve eggs separately (each one will take two minutes), then pare them nicely, and serve crown-shaped on a dish, putting a piece of fried bread between every other one. Pour over half a pint of reduced Espagnole (No. 105), to which has been added the zest of a lemon, and six sliced mushrooms, and serve very hot.

## 19. *Eggs en Filets.*

Mix in a dish that may be put in the oven (a silver one by prefer-ence) twelve raw egg yolks, with a spoonful of brandy and a pinch of salt. Cook them for five minutes in a hot oven, then let them cool; cut the preparation into twelve thin fillets or slices, and steep each one in a light pancake batter. Fry them in very hot fat for about two minutes, then lift up with a skimmer, lay them on a napkin to drain, and serve on a folded napkin laid on a hot dish and garnished with fried parsley.

## 20. *Eggs à la Finoise.*

Pour a pint of good tomato sauce into a saucepan on the hot stove, add two cut-up, peeled, sweet peppers, fry for two minutes in a tablespoonful of butter, a teaspoonful of chopped chives, and reduce it gradually to about half the quantity, which will take ten minutes. Poach six very fresh eggs, as for No. 1, pare their edges neatly. Place six freshly prepared hot toasts on a warm serving-dish, arrange the eggs carefully on top, and pour the above sauce over all, then send them to the table at once.

## 21. *Eggs au Miroir.*

Lightly butter a silver dish large enough to hold twelve eggs, one beside another; carefully break into it twelve eggs, taking care to keep the yolks intact. Evenly sprinkle over them half a pinch of salt. Cook for one minute on a hot stove; then place them in the oven for one and a half minutes. Take out, and place the dish on another, and serve.

## 22. *Eggs with Fresh Mushrooms*

Peel, wash, and drain a quarter of a pound of fine, fresh mushrooms. Place them in a saucepan, with a tablespoonful of very good butter. Season with half a pinch of salt and a third of a pinch of white pepper, squeezing in first two drops of lemon juice. Cover the saucepan, and cook for ten minutes on a moderate fire. Add a quarter of a glassful of good Madeira wine; reduce to one-half, which will take two minutes; add now a gill of béchamel sauce (No. 108), and let come to a boil again. Prepare twelve fresh-poached eggs, as in No. 1; pour the sauce on a hot serving-dish, keeping the mushrooms in the saucepan. Neatly lay the eggs over the sauce around the dish, and dress the mushrooms right in the centre, and serve very hot.

## 23. *Eggs with Celery*.

Boil for fifteen minutes, in a quart of white broth (No. 101 ), two heads of well-washed and neatly pared, sound celery. Remove it from the broth; then cut it up in one-inch-length pieces, and return it to the pan with the broth in which it was first boiled, leaving it on the hot stove. Season with one pinch of salt and the third of a pinch of white pepper. Reduce to three-quarters (which will require ten minutes). Add a gill of hot béchamel sauce (No. 108), let come to a boil. Poach twelve fresh eggs exactly as in No. 1, neatly arrange them on a hot dish, crown-like. Pour the celery sauce right in the centre, and serve very hot.

## 24. *Eggs with Truffles.*

Peel three medium-sized, sound truffles. Cut them into thin slices, place in a saucepan with a glassful of Madeira wine; reduce to one-half on a moderate fire. Season with one pinch of salt and the third of a pinch of white pepper; add one gill of béchamel sauce (No. 108); let come to a boil. Prepare twelve heart-shaped croûtons (No. 102); dip the thin parts first into the sauce half an inch in depth, then into fresh, finely chopped-up parsley up to the same depth. Gently dress (arrange) them on the hot serving-dish in star-shape, so that the decorated ends of the croûtons will just reach up to the edge of the dish equally all around. Prepare twelve poached eggs exactly the same as in No. 1; dress an egg on each croûton. Gently pour the above prepared sauce right in the centre of the dish, being careful not to pour any over the eggs. Evenly slice one good-sized, sound truffle into twelve equal slices; dip them in a little hot broth for two seconds; lay one slice on top of each egg, and serve immediately.

## 25. *Eggs with Tarragon.*

Blanch for one minute in a sautoire a quarter of a bunch of tarragon-leaves, drain, and chop them up very fine. Break twelve eggs into a bowl, add the tarragon, season with a pinch of salt and half a pinch of pepper, and beat well for four minutes; meanwhile adding half a cupful of sweet cream. Then make an omelet, as for No. 46, and roll it on a hot serving-dish. Prepare a little roux with flour and butter (No. 109), moisten with half a pint of strong broth and a glassful of white wine; skim off any fat that may accumulate on top, and let it cook slowly for ten minutes. Strain through a fine sieve and pour it around the omelet; then serve.

## 26. *Eggs with Livers.*

Remove the gall carefully from about a pint of chicken livers, wash them well, drain, and slice them into small pieces. Place them in a sautoire with one ounce of butter; range the pan on the hot stove, then season with one pinch of salt and half a pinch of pepper; toss the contents gently for two minutes; then add a pinch of chopped parsley, one pinch of chervil, and three well-minced mushrooms, and moisten with half a pint of Madeira sauce (No. 103); and let cook for five minutes; make an omelet of twelve eggs, as for No. 46, and when ready to finish, pour the livers in the centre, reserving two tablespoonfuls of it for further action; close the sides up carefully, cook two seconds longer, then gently turn it on a hot dish, and, with a spoon, pour all the sauce around the omelet. Dress the livers that were reserved, at both ends of the omelet, equally divided, and serve.

## 27. *Eggs au Parmesan.*

Beat twelve eggs in a saucepan, with two tablespoonfuls of grated Parmesan cheese, a pinch of pepper, but no salt ; stir them well with a whip, and make of this six small omelets, as for No. 46. As soon as they are sufficiently firm, lay them on a dish. Besprinkle the tops with a little grated Parmesan cheese, roll, and trim them nicely, sprinkle more cheese over the tops, wipe off the sides of the dish, and put them in a hot oven for five minutes. Remove from the oven, pour around the omelets one gill of hot Madeira sauce (No. 103), and serve very hot.

## 28. *Eggs à la Bonne Femme.*

Slice two large, sound onions, and fry them in two ounces of butter, in a saucepan, stirring frequently, so that they do not burn ; when done, dredge in a good pinch of flour, moistening with half a pint of cream or milk, and season with a pinch of salt, half a pinch of pepper, and a saltspoonful of nutmeg.  Break six eggs, froth the whites, mix the yolks with the onions, and afterward the beaten whites, stirring well.  Lay two pieces of white paper on the bottom of a baking-tin, butter them thoroughly, lay the eggs on top, and set it in the oven for about fifteen minutes.  When done, turn them on to a hot dish, remove the papers, add two tablespoonfuls of Espagnole sauce (No. 105) to the eggs and serve.

## 29. *Eggs à la Paysanne.*

Put half a pint of cream into a dish, on the fire, and when it boils, break in twelve fresh eggs, season with a pinch of salt and twelve whole peppers ; let cook for two minutes, and then set it in the oven for three minutes, so that the eggs get a good golden color, taking care that they do not harden. Remove from the oven, place the dish on another, and serve.

34

## 30. *Eggs à la Régence.*

Shred an ounce and a half of salt pork into fine pieces (ham will answer the same purpose), also one onion cut into small squares, and six medium-sized mushrooms, all of equal size ; moisten with a spoonful of good gravy, and cook for five minutes. When done, reduce with a tablespoonful of mushroom essence (liquor). Break twelve fresh eggs in a dish, with an ounce of melted butter on the bottom, and set it in a moderate oven for five minutes ; pour the garnishing over, drip off the fat, wipe the sides of the dish, and add six drops of strong tarragon-vinegar. Remove from the oven, place the dish on another, and serve.

## 31. *Eggs with Melted Cheese.*

Grate two ounces of Parmesan cheese on a dish ; set it on a slow fire, adding half a glassful of white wine, a pinch of chopped parsley, a pinch of chopped chives, half a pinch of pepper, and a saltspoonful of grated nutmeg, also two ounces of good butter. Stir thoroughly while cooking, and as the cheese melts, break in twelve eggs ; cook for five minutes longer, then surround the dish with heart-shaped croûtons (No. 102) set it on another dish, and serve very hot.

## 32. *Eggs en Panade*.

Cut out twelve round pieces of bread-crumbs, each one measuring two inches in diameter, and place them in a pie-plate, spreading a little butter over each ; brown them in the hot oven for one minute. Break twelve eggs in a bowl, add one pinch of chopped parsley, half a pinch of chives, two tablespoonfuls of thick, sweet cream, one ounce of butter, a pinch of salt, and a very little white pepper. Beat sharply all together for four minutes. Add the twelve pieces of browned bread to the beaten eggs ; mix them well together. Place in a frying-pan on the hot range one ounce of clarified butter, heat thoroughly, then fry one egged bread at a time for one and a half minutes on each side. Dress, with the aid of a cake-turner on a hot dish with a folded napkin ; keep in a warm place. Repeat the same process with the others, and serve.

## 33. *Eggs à la Meyerbeer*.

Butter a silver dish and break into it twelve fresh eggs ; or, if desired, use six small silver dishes, breaking two eggs into each one ; then cook them on the stove for two minutes.    Cut six mutton kidneys in halves, broil or stew them according to taste, then add them to the eggs, and serve with half a pint of hot Périgueux sauce (No. 110) thrown over.

## 34.  *Eggs à la Reine.*

Prepare twelve eggs as for No. 33, cook them for two minutes. Make a garnishing of one ounce of cooked chicken-breast, one finely shred, medium-sized truffle, and six minced mushrooms.  Moisten with half a pint of good Allemande sauce (No. 111), heat it up well, but do not let it boil ; then pour over the eggs and serve immediately.

## 35. *Eggs à la Turque.*

Cook twelve eggs the same as for No. 33, and pour over them six chicken livers, tossed gently but rapidly in a saucepan on a brisk fire with one ounce of butter for three minutes, and then with a spoon remove all the butter from the saucepan. Season with a pinch of salt, and half a pinch of white pepper, adding half a glass of good Madeira wine. Reduce it to one half, then add one gill of hot Madeira sauce (No. 103), heat up a little, and then pour the sauce over the eggs and serve.

### 36. *Eggs à l'Impératrice.*

Cook twelve eggs exactly as in No. 33, arranging six small slices of pâté-de-foie-gras, one on top of each egg, and serving very hot.

### 37. *Eggs à la Suisse.*

Fry twelve eggs as for No. 33 ; after cooking for two minutes, cover with half a pint of hot tomato sauce, and add three cooked sausages, cut in two, also a little grated cheese, then send to the table.

## 38. *Eggs à la Chipolata.*

Prepare twelve eggs as for No. 33, and cover them with a pint of hot Chipolata garnishing (No. 112), and serve very hot.

## 39. *Eggs à l'Alsacienne.*

Fry twelve eggs as for No. 33, only putting them on a long dish. Add one chopped onion to four ounces of finely minced calf's liver, quickly toss them on a brisk fire for about eight minutes, then pour in about six to eight drops of vinegar, a pinch of salt, and a little pepper to season. Garnish both ends of the dish with this, then serve.

## 40. *Eggs à l'Aurore.*

Boil twelve eggs until hard, then let them cool ; shell them, and separate the yolks from the whites, putting the former into a mortar, adding one ounce of fresh butter, a pinch of salt, half a pinch of nutmeg, the same of ground spice, and three raw egg yolks ; pound all well together. Mince the whites, and put them in a sautoire with a pint of well reduced béchamel (No. 108), cook without boiling, although letting them attain a good consistency ; place them on the dish used for serving, lay the pounded yolks on top, and garnish with twelve square sippets of bread dipped in beaten egg, and put in the oven to brown for about four minutes ; then serve.

43

## 41. *Eggs à la Polonaise.*

Cut twelve hard-boiled eggs in halves, separate the whites from the yolks, and pound the latter in a mortar, adding about one ounce of butter, a pinch of salt, half a pinch of ground spice, a saltspoonful of grated nutmeg, and five raw yolks ; when well blended, without any lumps, strew half a tablespoonful of very fine chopped parsley over, and add the whites of the five eggs well beaten. Garnish the bottom of a baking-dish with this preparation, laying it in about a finger thick ; also fill the whites with a part of it, making them have the appearance of whole eggs. Arrange them tastefully on top, and set the dish in the oven ; brown slightly for about five minutes, remove it from the oven, lay the dish on top of another, wipe the sides carefully, and serve immediately.

44

## 42.  *Eggs à la Sauce Robert.*

Peel two medium-sized onions, and remove the hearts, cut them in slices (the hearts), and put them with a tablespoonful of butter in a saucepan on a brisk fire, and brown them well. Moisten with a cupful of lean broth, season with a pinch of salt and half a pinch of pepper, cook, and let the sauce reduce for about ten minutes.   When ready to serve, cut eight hard-boiled eggs into slices, mix them in the preparation, and let heat together without boiling for two minutes ; finish with a teaspoonful of diluted mustard, and then serve.

## 43. *Eggs à la Hyde.*

Boil six fresh eggs for seven minutes, then lay them in cold water for five minutes to cool them off; shell them, and put them on a plate. Hash fine half a small canful of mushrooms with two branches of parsley and one medium-sized, sound shallot. Put in a saucepan on the hot stove one ounce of good butter, and when melted add the prepared mushrooms, and let cook rather slowly for fifteen minutes, stirring it occasionally. Add half a pint of Madeira sauce (No. 103), season with a pinch of salt and a light pinch of pepper, then cook again slowly for ten minutes. Strain the whole through a fine sieve into another saucepan, and set it aside to keep warm ; cut the six hard-boiled eggs into halves, remove the entire yolks, and mash them thoroughly in a bowl, adding half an ounce of good, fresh butter and half a pint of sweet cream. Season with a light pinch of salt, half a pinch of pepper, and half a teaspoonful of grated nutmeg ; mix well together, and with this fill the twelve pieces of egg-white. Lay them on a lightly buttered dish, pour the sauce over, and put them in the oven for eight minutes before sending to the table.

## 44. *Eggs à la Bennett.*

Cut twelve hard-boiled eggs lengthwise, remove the yolks, and place them in a bowl with two ounces of good butter, a teaspoonful of anchovy essence, and a pinch of chopped chives. Beat well together, and fill the whites with it, besprinke with bread-crumbs, and pour over a few drops of clarified butter; put them in the oven for three minutes on a buttered dish, and serve with half a pint of hot Madeira sauce (No. 103) thrown over.

## 45. *Eggs à la Duchesse.*

Place a quarter of a pound of powdered sugar in a saucepan, adding half a pint of water, a small piece of lemon peel, and a short stick of cinnamon. Boil until the sugar is reduced to a syrup, then remove the lemon peel and cinnamon, and add half a teaspoonful of orange-flower water. Beat together, then strain twelve egg yolks with a pint of milk or cream, add this to the syrup with a very little salt, then transfer the whole to a silver baking-dish, place it on the hot stove, and let cook for ten minutes, stirring briskly, and when it forms a cream, squeeze in the juice of a fine, sound lemon ; remove from the fire, lay the dish on another, and send to the table.

49

## 46. *Plain Omelet*.

Crack into a bowl twelve fresh eggs, season them with a pinch of salt and half a pinch of white pepper, beat them well until the whites and yolks are thoroughly mixed, or for fully four minutes. Place in a No. 8 frying-pan two tablespoonfuls of clarified butter ; heat it well on the hot range, and when it crackles pour in the eggs, and with a fork stir all well for two minutes, then let rest for half a minute. Fold up with the fork—the side nearest the handle first—to the centre of the omelet, then the opposite side, so that both sides will meet right in the centre ; let rest for half a minute longer ; have a hot dish in the left hand, take hold of the handle of the pan with the right, bring both dish and pan to a triangular shape, and with a rapid movement turn the pan right over the centre of the dish, and send to the table. (The omelet should be made on a very brisk range, without taking the lid off the stove.)

Should the pan be smaller than the above-mentioned No. 8 it will require three minutes' stirring, one minute to rest, and half a minute to rest after having been folded.

When making an omelet for one person, for instance, use three fresh eggs, seasoned with half a teaspoonful of salt, and half a salt-spoonful of white pepper. Thoroughly heat in a small frying-pan half a teaspoonful of clarified butter ; after sharply beating the eggs in the bowl, pour into the pan, and gently mix for one minute on a very brisk range, let rest for a quarter of a minute, fold one side up, rest a quarter of a minute more, then turn on a small hot dish, and serve.

51

## 47. *Omelet with Fine Herbs.*

Break twelve fresh eggs into a bowl, add a pinch of finely chopped parsley, half a pinch of chopped tarragon, and half a pinch of chives; also, if desired, half a cupful of sweet cream. Beat the whole thoroughly without stopping for four minutes; melt one ounce of good butter in a frying-pan on the hot stove; when it is melted and begins to crackle, pour in the eggs, and mix them gently with a fork, while they cook for three minutes : let them rest for one minute, then bring the sides toward the centre, turn it on a hot dish, and serve.

## 48.  *Oyster  Omelet.*

Blanch eighteen oysters to boiling point in their own water ; drain, and return them to the saucepan, moistening with half a pint of good Allemande (No. 111) ; season with half a pinch of salt.  Make a plain omelet with twelve eggs as for No. 46, bring the sides toward the centre, and fill it with the oyster preparation.  Turn it on a hot dish, pour the rest of the sauce around, and serve very hot.

## 49. *Crawfish Omelet.*

Stew twelve crawfish tails in a sautoire on the hot stove with half an ounce of butter, letting them cook for five minutes. Break twelve eggs into a bowl, add half a cupful of sweet cream, and a pinch of finely chopped parsley ; season with a pinch of salt and half a pinch of pepper, then sharply beat for four minutes. Make an omelet as in No. 46, fold up the side opposite the handle of the pan, place the crawfish right in the centre, fold up the other side, turn it on a hot dish, and serve.

## 50. *Lobster Omelet.*

Take six ounces of boiled lobster meat, and cut it into small pieces; put them into a sautoire with half a glassful of white wine and a quarter of an ounce of butter. Moisten with a quarter of a pint of strong, hot béchamel (No. 108), and let cook for five minutes. Make an omelet of twelve eggs as for No. 46, and with a skimmer place the stewed lobster in the middle, fold the opposite side, pour in the garnishing, fold the other side up, turn it on a hot dish, pour the sauce around it, and serve

## 51. *Tomato Omelet.*

Break twelve fresh eggs in a bowl, season them with a pinch of salt and half a pinch of pepper, and beat thoroughly for four minutes. Place two ounces of butter in a frying-pan on a hot stove, let it heat well without browning, then pour into it half a pint of freshly cooked stewed tomatoes, suppressing all the liquid. Cook for two minutes, then throw the beaten eggs over, and with a fork mix the whole gently for three minutes; let rest for one minute longer. Bring up the two opposite sides, turn it carefully on a hot dish, and serve.

## 52. *Tomato Omelet à la Provençale.*

Peel a medium-sized, sound onion, then chop it fine ; place it in a sautoire on the hot stove with one ounce of butter, and let get a good golden color, adding half a pint of stewed tomatoes, or two good-sized, peeled raw tomatoes cut into small slices, a crushed clove of garlic, and season (should the tomatoes be fresh) with a pinch of salt and half a pinch of pepper, adding a teaspoonful of chopped parsley; let the whole cook together for ten minutes; then proceed as for the tomato omelet (No. 51).

### 53. *Asparagus-top Omelet.*

Put a quarter of a bunch of boiled asparagus-tops into a bowl, pour twelve beaten eggs over, season with a pinch of salt and half a pinch of pepper, mix lightly again, and make an omelet exactly as for No. 46.

### 54. *Omelet, with Green Peas.*

Break twelve eggs into a bowl, adding half a pint of boiled green peas, a pinch each of salt and pepper, beat well for four minutes, and make into an omelet as for No. 46.

## 55. *Omelet au Cèpes.*

Fry six cèpes, cut into small pieces, in half an ounce of butter for two minutes. Beat twelve eggs in a bowl, season with a pinch of salt and half a pinch of pepper, pour them over the cèpes, and make an omelet as for No. 46.

## 56. *Smoked Beef Omelet.*

Fry two ounces of finely minced, smoked beef in a frying-pan, with half an ounce of butter, add twelve well-beaten eggs, and make an omelet as for No. 46.

## 57. *Ham Omelet.*

Cut about two ounces of lean ham into small, square pieces, fry them for two minutes with an ounce of butter in a frying-pan, and throw over twelve well-beaten eggs ; with this make an omelet as for No 46.

## 58. *Crab Omelet.*

Proceed exactly the same as for No. 50, substituting six ounces of crab meat cut into small pieces, for the lobster.

## 59. *Kidney Omelet.*

Stew on the hot stove three minced kidneys, with a quarter of a pint of Madeira wine sauce (No. 103), let cook for three minutes. Make a plain omelet with twelve eggs as for No. 46, fold the opposite side up, put the kidneys in the centre, fold the other side up, and turn on a dish, and pour the sauce around ; then serve.

## 60. *Chicken Liver Omelet.*

The same as for the above (No. 59), substituting six minced chicken livers for the kidneys.

## 61. *Sausage Omelet.*

Skin three raw sausages, then put them in a saucepan with a quarter of an ounce of butter; set it on the hot fire for five minutes, and stir well until they cook. Make a plain omelet with twelve eggs, as for No. 46, fold the opposite side, lay the sausages in the centre, fold the other side up, and serve with a quarter of a pint of hot Madeira sauce (No. 103), poured around the omelet.

## 62. *Omelet Bonne Femme.*

Cut one ounce of salt pork into small square pieces, also two tablespoonfuls of crust from off a fresh loaf of bread cut the same way; fry them together in a frying-pan with an ounce of butter for about two minutes, adding a boiled potato cut into small squares, a pinch of chopped parsley, half a pinch of chopped chives, half a pinch of salt, and the same quantity of pepper. Beat twelve eggs for four minutes in a bowl, pour them into the pan, and make an omelet as for No. 46; turn on a hot dish, and serve.

63

## 63. *Omelet Raspail.*

Chop one raw onion very fine, and put it in a saucepan with an ounce of butter. Take one ounce of small squares of salt pork, cook them slightly, adding an ounce of scraps of very finely minced, cooked roast beef, the same of ham, two finely chopped mushrooms, and a pinch of chopped parsley. Stir in well a tablespoonful of tomato sauce and a tablespoonful of grated bread crumbs ; season with a pinch of pepper and third of a pinch of salt. Make a plain omelet with twelve eggs as for No. 46, fold up the opposite side, fill it with the preparation, fold the other side up, turn it on a hot dish, and serve.

## 64. *Sardine Omelet.*

Thoroughly skin eight fine sardines, place six of them in a frying-pan with an ounce of butter, cook for two minutes. Beat well twelve eggs in a bowl. Season with one pinch of salt and half a pinch of pepper, add them to the sardines in the pan; make an omelet as in No. 46, fold the opposite end up, place the two remaining sardines right in the centre, fold the other end up, turn it on a hot dish, and send to the table.

## 65. Cheese Omelet.

Put one ounce of butter in a frying-pan, heat it on the hot stove. Break twelve eggs into a bowl, beat them thoroughly for four minutes, adding two tablespoonfuls of grated Swiss cheese, half a pinch of salt, and half a pinch of pepper. Pour the whole into the frying-pan, and make an omelet as for No. 46; turn it on a hot dish, and besprinkle the top lightly with a very little Parmesan cheese; place in the oven for two seconds, then serve.

## 66. *Omelet Régence*.

Make an omelet with twelve eggs as for No. 46, and when nearly cooked, fold up the opposite side, then fill the centre with a quarter of a pint of hot Régence garnishing (No. 30), fold the other side up; turn on a hot dish, pour the sauce around, and serve hot.

## 67. *Omelet à la Vanderbilt.*

Take two fine, sound, green peppers, plunge them into hot fat for half a minute, then take them up and lay them on a dry cloth; skin them neatly, remove all the seeds from the insides, and when emptied cut them into small slices. Put these into a saucepan on the hot stove with two medium-sized fresh, sound, sliced tomatoes, twelve nicely shelled shrimps, and three tablespoonfuls of Madeira wine sauce (No. 103), then season with half a pinch of salt and a third of a pinch of pepper; cook slowly for fifteen minutes. Break twelve fresh eggs into a bowl, season them with half a pinch of salt and a third of a pinch of pepper, and beat well for five minutes. Put two ounces of good butter in a frying-pan, place it on the hot stove, and when the butter is melted drop in the eggs, and with a spoon or fork mix briskly for two minutes. Fold the opposite side up with a skimmer, lift up the thick part of the prepared sauce, and place it in the centre of the omelet, fold the other side either with a knife or fork, and let it cook for two minutes longer, then turn on a hot dish; pour the rest of the sauce in the saucepan around the omelet, and send to the table very hot.

## 68. *Omelet à l'Espagnole.*

Put in a stewpan on the stove one finely shred onion, one ounce of butter, a chopped green pepper; six minced mushrooms, and one large, finely cut-up tomato; season with half a pinch of pepper and one pinch of salt, adding a spoonful of tomato sauce; let cook for fifteen minutes. Make a plain omelet with twelve eggs, as for No. 46, fold the opposite side, and put more than half of the stew inside of it, say three-quarters; fold the other side up, and turn it on a long dish, then pour the rest of the sauce around, and serve.

## 69. *Omelet Mexicaine.*

Have a pint of velouté sauce (No. 115) in a saucepan, place it on a moderate fire, add a piece of lobster butter (No. 116) about the size of an egg, twenty-four shelled and cooked shrimps, and season with half a pinch of salt and a very little pepper. Let cook for three minutes, stirring it lightly, then add half of a good-sized, empty and peeled green pepper, finely hashed; cook for two minutes longer, then let rest on the corner of the stove. Make an omelet with twelve eggs, as for No. 46, fold up the opposite side, pour half of the preparation in the centre, fold the other end up, turn the omelet on a hot dish, and garnish both sides with the rest of the shrimps, pouring the balance around the dish: then send to the table.

## 70. Sweet Omelet.

Beat and sweeten with one ounce of sugar twelve eggs; make an omelet as for No. 46, using one ounce of fresh butter; turn it on a dish, and dredge another ounce of sugar over, then glaze it with a hot shovel or salamander, and serve very warm.

### 71. *Omelet Soufflée, for Six Persons.*

Have a deep, cold, silver dish ready, fifteen inches long by eleven wide. Put into a vessel four ounces of powdered sugar. Break twelve fresh eggs, drop the whites into a copper basin, and the yolks of five into the vessel containing the sugar, reserving the other seven yolks for other purposes. Add to the vessel containing the sugar and yolks a light teaspoonful of vanilla essence: now with the wooden spatula, begin to beat the yolks with the sugar as briskly as you possibly can for fifteen minutes. Lay it aside. Then with the aid of a pastry wire-whip, beat up to a very stiff froth the twelve egg whites in the copper basin, which will take from twelve to fifteen minutes. Remove the pastry wire-whip; take a skimmer in the right hand, and with the left take hold of the vessel containing the preparation of the yolks and sugar. Gradually pour it over the whites, and with the skimmer gently mix the whole together for two minutes. The preparation will now be of a light, firm consistency. Now, with the aid again of the skimmer, take up the preparation and drop it down in the centre of the cold dish, ready as above mentioned, taking special care to pile it as high as possible, so as to have it of a perfect dome-shape; a few incisions can be made all around, according to taste; immediately place it in a moderate oven to bake for fifteen minutes. Take it out of the oven, and, in order to avoid burning or soiling the table-cloth, lay the dish containing the omelet on another cold one, liberally sprinkle powdered sugar over it, and immediately send to the table.

N. B.—Special care should be taken when piling the preparation into the cold, silver dish; and the making of the incisions should be done as rapidly as possible, so that success will be certain. When desired, the vanilla essence can be substituted with the same quantity of orange-flower water.

## 72. Omelet au Kirsch, or Rum.

Make a sweet omelet with twelve eggs as for No. 70; when completed and glazed, throw around it a glassful of kirsch, and set the omelet on fire; serve it while burning. Rum omelet is prepared exactly the same way, substituting rum for kirsch.

74

## 73. Omelet Célestine.

Pulverize six macaroons, put them in a bowl, adding three table-spoonfuls of apple jelly and one spoonful of whipped cream; mix well with the spatula. Make a sweet omelet as for No. 70, with twelve eggs; fold the opposite side up, pour the mixture into the centre, fold the other end up, turn it on a hot dish, and sprinkle the top with three tablespoonfuls of powdered sugar; glaze the omelet with a hot shovel or salamander, and decorate it with three lady-fingers cut in two, also a cupful of whipped cream, the latter poured into a paper-funnel, and piped over in any design the fancy may dictate.

## 74. *Eggs à la W. B. Kendall.*

Have six medium-sized, thoroughly ripe, red and sound tomatoes, wash and dry them; cut away a piece an inch in diameter at the bottom of the tomatoes, including the stems; remove the seed with a vegetable scoop. Lightly butter a little sautoire, then gently lay the tomatoes in the pan, the cut part upward, mix one tablespoonful of salt with a teaspoonful of pepper, and with it equally season the inside of the tomatoes; sprinkle their surface with a little clarified butter, then place in a very hot oven for three minutes. Remove them from the oven, place the sautoire on a table, then crack one fresh egg into each tomato, place them in the oven again for two minutes, remove them.  Arrange six fried bread croûtons on a hot dish, then with the cake-turner take the tomatoes one by one and lay them over each croûton.  Chop up very fine one sound peeled shallot, one green pepper, and half a clove of sound garlic, place these in a sautoire with a tablespoonful of clarified butter, range the pan on the corner of the hot stove, and slowly simmer for four minutes, then add a gill of tomato sauce, and one drop of tabasco sauce; cook for three minutes.  Strain the same through a sieve into a hot bowl, sharply pressing the peppers with a wooden spoon.  Pour the sauce now around the tomatoes, but not on top of them, and send to the table.

## 75. *Eggs Molet.*

Take six fresh eggs, drop them all at the same time with a skimmer or a spoon into boiling water, and let boil for five minutes and a half, but no longer; lift them up, and immediately drop them into cold water for two minutes, then take them up carefully; peel them —seeing that the white is intact—then keep them in a little warm consommé or water. Have a quart of hot purée of chestnuts (No. 117), place it in a pastry-bag, in which you previously slide down a fancy tube, then nicely decorate the border of a silver dish, large enough to hold the six eggs, also a little at the bottom to lay the eggs over. Place the dish in the hot oven for two minutes, then pour in the centre of the dish a gill of demi-glace sauce (No. 103); gently lay the eggs in the centre of the dish, and serve.

The above eggs can be served in various ways—with chicory garnishing, spinach, sorrel, Spanish sauce, plain, etc.

## 76. *Eggs à la Villeroi.*

Take three fresh, hard boiled eggs, cut each one into half, length-wise, remove the yolks, and chop up the latter very fine, leaving the whites on a plate for further action. Chop up very fine one medium-sized sound truffle, one ounce of cooked smoked beef tongue—the red part by preference. Place these in a sautoire with a tablespoonful of Madeira wine, reduce on the hot range until almost dry, then add the chopped-up yolks, and a tablespoonful of poulette sauce (No. 118). Season with a tablespoonful of salt and a teaspoonful of pepper, mix all well together. Then stuff the six half egg whites with the prepara-tion evenly divided, and giving them an oval shape. Have a gill of poulette sauce (No. 118), then with a fork steep each egg in it, so as to completely cover them with the sauce. Place them on a dish and let cool off. Beat up an egg in a bowl with two tablespoonfuls cold milk, gently roll the eggs in it, then roll them in fresh bread-crumbs. Fry them in very hot fat for five minutes. Take them up with a skim-mer, dress on a hot dish with a folded napkin, and serve with a gill of cream sauce (No. 119) in a bowl separate.

## 77. *Eggs à la Buckley.*

Take six hard boiled eggs, cut them in halves crosswise, take out the yolks, place them in a bowl, then with a spoon mash them with an ounce of good butter, season with a teaspoonful of salt and half a teaspoonful of pepper, add a teaspoonful of freshly chopped chives, and a teaspoonful of chopped parsley, one tablespoonful of cold milk, and two tablespoonfuls of very fresh bread-crumbs. Mix the whole well together with a spoon, then with the preparation fill the hollow space of the twelve half eggs just even up to the surface. Close them together so as to give them their original shape. Then carefully press a skewer through one egg, right in the centre lengthwise, then another, so as to have two on each skewer, repeat the same with the other four.

Lay them in a sautoire with a gill of white broth (No. 101). Cover the sautoire with either a copper or tin cover, and place in the oven for five minutes. Remove them; have a hot dish ready with three canapés. Arrange the skewers over each canapé, and serve with the following sauce:

Cut into small dice-shaped pieces four mushrooms, one good-sized sound truffle, and one ounce of cooked chicken breast; place these in a sautoire with half a wine-glassful of white wine. Reduce it on the range for three minutes, or until almost dry, then add a gill of poulette sauce (No. 118). Continually stir until very hot, but do not allow it to boil. Now pour the sauce around the eggs on the canapés, but not over them, then serve.

## 78. *Eggs à la Jay Gould.*

Prepare in a sautoire two ounces of good butter, half a gill of Allemande sauce (No. 111), three tablespoonfuls of grated Parmesan cheese and one tablespoonful of white broth (No. 101). Place on the hot range and stir until the cheese is thoroughly dissolved, then place the pan on the corner of the range to keep warm. Take six hard boiled shelled eggs. Cut each one into four even slices crosswise, season with a tablespoonful of salt and a teaspoonful of pepper equally divided. Lightly butter a silver dish. Arrange a very thin layer of the above garnishing over it. Take the sliced eggs and lay one slice on the dish, then a very small thin slice of Swiss cheese—then again

82

a slice of egg and a slice of cheese—always keeping them one over-lapping another, both eggs and cheese; continue the same with the rest, giving a crown shape around the dish.

Pour half a gill of hot tomato sauce on top of both eggs and cheese, equally divided. Now pour the balance of the garnishing over all, also equally divided; lightly sprinkle the top with a very little clarified butter, and then place in a brisk oven for eight minutes, so that it should get a good brown color. Remove from out the oven and serve immediately.

## 79. *Eggs à la W. M. Evarts.*

Have six hard boiled shelled eggs, carefully cut away the third part of each egg on the surface. Remove the yolks without breaking the whites, leave the whites on a plate until further action: thoroughly mash the yolks in a bowl with a spoon; add a teaspoonful of grated Parmesan cheese, a tablespoonful of Allemande sauce (No. 111), half a teaspoonful of anchovy sauce. Season with one tablespoonful of salt and half a teaspoonful of pepper. Knead all well together, then fill the inside of the eggs with the preparation, and giving them an oval shape a quarter of an inch over the surface. Cut three of the six pieces into small strips lengthwise, a quarter of an inch thick, gently lay one strip over each egg crosswise—right in the centre, so that, when completed, they will represent small fancy baskets. Neatly decorate their surface with a little cooked jardinière; arranged in this way they will represent perfect baskets of abundance. Arrange a small layer of the preparation for each egg on a silver dish just wide enough to hold each one firmly. Place the eggs now on top of each layer, pour a gill of Colbert sauce (No. 120) around the dish, but none over the eggs. Cover them with a piece of well-buttered paper, then place in the oven—rather moderate—for two minutes. Take from out the oven and immediately send to the table.

## 80. *Eggs à la Geo. O. Jones.*

Take six shelled hard boiled eggs, cut away at the pointed end of each egg a piece half an inch thick, and at the other end a quarter of an inch thick. Remove the yolks with a small vegetable scoop, or with a pointed knife, mash the yolks in a bowl very fine, and lay them aside for further action.

Place in a sautoire half an ounce of good butter, add one sound shelled finely chopped shallot, place the pan on the corner of the range, and let simmer, but do not let get brown, add then a tablespoonful of Béchamel sauce (No. 108), a teaspoonful of freshly chopped up parsley, a tablespoonful of finely grated horse-radish. Now add also the yolks, season with a tablespoonful of salt and half a saltspoonful of Cayenne pepper; mix all well together with a wooden spoon, and then with it stuff the six eggs, so as to give them the exact shape of small barrels.

Lightly butter a tin pan, carefully lay the eggs in it, the stuffed part uppermost, sprinkle a little grated Parmesan cheese right in the centre of the stuffed part of the eggs. Cover them with a piece of buttered paper, place them in a moderate oven for twelve minutes. Carefully remove them from the oven, take off the paper. Have a hot dish with six fried bread croûtons, half an inch high by one and a half inches in diameter, gently place an egg on each croûton; pour a gill of hot demi-glace (No. 103) around the dish (none over the eggs) and immediately serve.

## 81. *Eggs à la A. F. Bowers.*

Peel a quarter of a pound of fine, fresh, sound mushrooms, wash them thoroughly, seeing that no sand remains on; lay six of the largest aside (with their stem cut away) for further action. Place in a sautoire one ounce of butter, two tablespoonfuls of flour; place this pan on the corner of a hot range, and let gently cook for eight minutes, slightly stirring once in a while. Add now the mushrooms, season with a tablespoonful of salt and half a teaspoonful of pepper, also half a saltspoonful of grated nutmeg, squeezing in the juice of a quarter of a sound lemon; mix all well together, then add a gill of milk, and let cook for five minutes, lightly stirring meanwhile. Strain through a fine sieve into a bowl, and keep it in a warm place until further action.

Have six shelled hard boiled eggs, and with the point of a keen knife make eight triangular incisions right in the centre of each egg down to the yolk, then with hands gently pull them apart. Remove the yolks, and mash them very fine, then well mix the latter with the preparation, and then with it stuff the eggs, giving them a dome shape. Lightly butter a silver dish, place a thin layer of the preparation over it. Firmly lay the six large mushrooms upside down over the layer, place half a teaspoonful of the force in the centre of each mushroom, then gently lay the eggs perpendicular over each mushroom. Slice a small truffle into six thin slices, place one on top of each egg, sprinkle a little clarified butter over all, cover them with buttered paper, then place in a moderate oven for fifteen minutes. Remove and serve with a gill of hot demi-glace (No. 103), in a bowl separate.

## 82. *Eggs à la Hamilton Fish.*

Cut up into very small dice shaped pieces, one. medium sized sound truffle, an ounce of cooked smoked beef tongue, and four mushrooms. Place them in a sautoire on the range, with half a glass of Madeira wine. Reduce the wine to one half, add now a gill of Madeira sauce (No. 103), and a drop of anchovy sauce, then cook for five minutes.

Take six shelled hard boiled eggs, cut them into halves lengthwise, remove the yolks, chop them up very fine, and add them to the sauce; mix all well together, and with this preparation stuff the whites. Close them together, place them in a lightly buttered sautoire, pour into it two tablespoonfuls of white broth (No. 101). Cover them with a sheet of buttered paper, and then place in the oven for eight minutes.

Have a hot dish, arrange six fried bread croûtons over it.    Take the eggs from out the oven, and place one on each croûton.

Plunge six small anchovies into hot water, take them up and dry well, arrange one around each egg in the centre, so as to represent a ring.

Cut up a medium-sized sound truffle into twelve small slices, triangular shape, then place one slice on top of the egg right in the centre on each side of the anchovy, proceed the same with the rest.

Pour a gill of hot Colbert sauce (No. 120), in the centre of the dish, but not over the eggs, and then send to the table.

## 83. *Eggs à la Darling.*

Provide one dozen of very tender, sound celery knots, peel and thoroughly wash them twice. Cut them in quarters, then place them in a saucepan with one ounce of butter, a quart of white broth (No. 101), a sprig of thyme, three cloves and twenty whole peppers, place the pan on the hot range and cook for sixty minutes. Strain through a sieve into another saucepan, seeing that everything is strained except the cloves and peppers. Dilute a teaspoonful of corn starch into half a cup of cold milk, and gradually add it to the purée, sharply stirring meanwhile. Cook for three minutes longer. Have six shelled hard boiled eggs ready, then place the purée right in the centre of a hot dish, giving it a dome shape. Gently arrange the six eggs around it, leaning slightly against the dome as a support to the column. Lay a thin slice of truffle in the centre of each, then pour a gill of hot Madeira sauce (No. 103), around the dish, but not over the eggs, and then serve.

## 84. *Eggs à la Mme. Morton.*

Carefully crack six fresh eggs on a saucer; heat in a frying-pan on the hot stove one tablespoonful of clarified butter, then drop in one egg and fry for two minutes, lift it up with a palette knife, carefully lay it on a hot dish, and continue the same with the other five.

Prepare six well designed round bread croûtons as for No. 102. Lay a very thin slice, the size of the croûton, of pâté-de-foie-gras over each croûton, and then with a round paste cutter, two inches and a half in diameter, place it right in the centre of each egg, taking special care to keep the yolks exactly in the centre, so as to cut away the white of each egg evenly from all around each yolk.   Place one egg on top of each croûton, pour a gill of hot Périgueux sauce (No. 110), around the eggs, but not over them, and serve.

## 85. *Eggs à la Belmont.*

Place in a sautoire eight well washed sound mushrooms, with half an ounce of butter, on the hot range, squeezing in just one drop of lemon juice, let gently simmer for three minutes; add a sound finely sliced up truffle, also half a wine-glassful of Madeira wine; let reduce to one half, which will take about three minutes, add then a gill of Espagnole sauce (No. 105) and cook for three minutes longer.

Prepare twelve small pâté-de-foie-gras balls the size of a Malaga grape, gently dip them in beaten egg, then in fresh bread-crumbs, and then fry them in very hot fat for two minutes, or until they obtain a good golden color, remove them with a skimmer, and lay them on a napkin to drain. Take up the mushrooms and truffles with a skimmer from the sauce, arrange them in two clusters, one at each end of the dish, as well as the twelve croquettes, also in clusters, six on each side of the dish.

Poach six very fresh eggs exactly as in No. 1. Cut out from an American bread six round croûtons, arrange them on the hot dish all around. Plunge into hot broth or consommé six artichoke bottoms, take them up and place one on each croûton. Pour the sauce right in the middle of the dish, but not over the eggs; place a slice of truffle on top of each egg, and serve.

## 86. *Eggs à la Mme. Diaz.*

Have three large sound green peppers, plunge them into very hot fat for two minutes, take them out, and with a coarse dry towel remove the skin of each; then cut each pepper into half, lengthwise, remove the seeds, have a frying pan on the hot range, two tablespoonfuls of either sweet oil or clarified butter. Cut six very thin slices of raw ham, place them gently in the pan, add the peppers also, and then gently cook for fifteen minutes. Prepare six pieces of dry toast, dress them on a hot dish, then place a slice of ham over each toast, then half a pepper over the ham.

Fry six very fresh eggs separately in clarified butter as for No. 84, and then gently place one on top of each pepper, and send to the table

## 87. *Eggs à la D. B. Hill.*

Carefully open (without losing any of their juice) into a bowl twelve medium sized fresh oysters; place them in a sautoire on the hot range, and let come to a boil, skim well, then strain the juice into a bowl, and keep the oysters in a separate bowl for further action.

Place in a pan one tablespoonful of very good butter with a table-spoonful of flour, mix well together with the spatula, then place it on the hot range and let slowly simmer for five minutes, taking care not to let get brown. Add now, little by little, the juice of the oysters, continually stirring meanwhile. Season with a teaspoonful of pepper. (If the oysters were not very salted, a little salt can be added.) Stir continually until it comes to a boil, and then let slowly cook for five minutes; add now six sliced mushrooms and the twelve oysters.

Lightly butter a deep silver dish, place the above sauce into it, then carefully crack in six fresh eggs; sprinkle a very little salt over them, sprinkle also the top with a very little clarified butter. Place them in the hot oven for two minutes. Remove from out the oven, decorate the dish with six heart-shaped bread croûtons, and serve.

## 88. *Eggs à la W. W. Ladd, Jr.*

Provide four fine, sound, white Kalamazoo celery. Cut away all the green leaves, and neatly trim it; thoroughly wash twice in cold water, so that no sand will adhere to the celery; cut the three celery, three inches long from the root part, crosswise. Place three pieces in a saucepan with one quart of white broth (No. 101). Season with half a tablespoonful of salt, four whole peppers, two cloves, and a sprig of thyme. Cover the pan, and let boil on the range for thirty minutes. Chop up very fine the balance of the celery, then place it in a small saucepan with one ounce of butter, let simmer for five minutes, add two tablespoonfuls of well sifted flour; stir well together, and cook for five minutes longer; gradually add now a cup of either hot or cold milk, stirring well without ceasing while adding it, and until it begins to boil; season with a tablespoonful of salt, and half a saltspoonful of Cayenne pepper, and cook for twenty minutes longer. Remove it from the range, press it through a sieve into a bowl. Well

98

butter a silver dish a foot and a quarter in length by three-quarters in width. Slide a tube into a pastry bag, pour the celery purée into it, and carefully press it down two inches from the centre of the dish, commencing at the side of the dish, coming down two inches and a half to the right, continuing going all around giving an oval shape; make another oval border over the other. Crack six fresh eggs in the centre inside the border, then place the dish in the hot oven for five minutes. Take up the celery from the pan, place on a dish, then split each one in two from the cut part down to the root only. Remove the eggs from the oven; open each celery triangular shape, place it jointly around the border so as to make it represent a star. Strain the broth in which the celery was cooked into a hot bowl, add to it a teaspoonful of freshly chopped parsley, mix a little, and then pour about a gill of it around the celery, but not over the eggs, and serve very hot.

## 89. *Eggs à la Cockrane.*

Take two sweet Spanish peppers, one ounce of cooked smoked beef tongue, cut them with a tube into slices the size of a cent, place them on a dish with six mushroom buttons until further action. Chop up very fine one sound peeled shallot, and put in a sautoire with a teaspoonful of butter, let cook for two minutes on the hot range. Chop up very fine the remainder of the tongue and Spanish peppers, place them in the sautoire with the shallot, moisten with a tablespoonful of Madeira wine, let simmer for one minute, then add half a gill of tomato sauce, and half a gill of Espagnole sauce (No. 105). Cook for two minutes. Add now the peppers, tongue, and mushrooms (which were laid on a dish) and let boil for one minute more. Arrange six fried bread croûtons on a hot dish. Poach six very fresh eggs as for No. 1, and place one egg on each croûton, then with a larding needle take up one mushroom from the pan, and lay it on the top of the egg right in the centre, then take up a piece of pepper, lay it on the right of the mushroom, lengthwise, and then take up a piece of tongue, and place it on the left of the mushrooms, and continue the same with the rest of the eggs. Pour the remaining sauce around the dish, but not over the eggs, and immediately send to the table.

## 90. *Eggs à la Lloyd Aspinwall.*

Take out from a can six large cêpes, lay them on a dish, and with a tube two inches in diameter, cut them perfectly round; place them in a sautoire on the range, with a tablespoonful of clarified butter and a finely chopped sound shallot; let cook for three minutes on a brisk fire, tossing well once in a while. Season with a tablespoonful of salt, a teaspoonful of pepper, adding the third of a clove of garlic finely chopped up; toss all well for one minute longer, and then lay the pan on the corner of the range. Have a deep silver dish lightly buttered; take up the six cêpes from the pan, arrange them nicely around the dish, place the dish at the oven door to keep warm.

Chop up very fine the remaining trimming of the cêpes, place them in the same pan in which the cêpes were cooked, add half a teaspoonful of freshly chopped parsley, squeeze in the juice of half a medium sized sound lemon, and a gill of Espagnole sauce (No. 105), and let the whole boil for one minute; pour the sauce all around the cêpes, but not over them. Crack a fresh egg over each cêpe, being careful not to break the yolk, sprinkle a little salt over each egg, place them in the hot oven for two minutes; remove them from out the oven, and immediately send to the table.

### 91. *Omelet Crême de Vanille à la R. A. C. Smith.*

Pour into a saucepan on the hot range two gills of fresh milk, add to it four ounces of powdered sugar, and also one vanilla bean, let come to a boil, take the pan from off the range, and let cool off. Remove the vanilla bean, dry it with a napkin, place it in a glass bottle with powdered sugar, cork it tightly, and use whenever necessary, as it will keep for any length of time. Add to the milk three heaped tablespoonfuls of *rice flour*—which can be had at Park & Tilford's—and with a wire whip thoroughly beat together, place the pan on the hot range, and continually stir until it boils, then place the pan on the corner of the range, and let cook slowly for twelve minutes; strain it through a very fine hair sieve into a bowl, add to it a teaspoonful of fresh butter, mix it thoroughly, and then leave it in a warm place for further action.

Make an omelet exactly as for No. 46, and just before folding the sides up place half of the preparation right in the centre, fold up, and gently turn it on a hot silver dish; place the rest of the preparation in a pastry bag, in which you previously slide down a small tube at the bottom, press down, make a small rose at each end of the omelet, dredge a little powdered sugar over the omelet, gently glaze it with a red iron, decorate the sides with any kind of dry cakes at hand, cut in triangular shape, and send to the table.

## 92. *Omelet à la Clark.*

Make preparation exactly the same as for No. 91, only substituting half a wineglass of Maraschino for the vanilla, and proceed with the rest precisely the same.

## 93. *Omelet Hughes.*

Have a preparation made the same as in No. 91, but using a teaspoonful of extract of orange flower, in place of the vanilla, proceed and serve the same.

### 94. Omelet à la E. L. Godkin.

Cut into quarters three fine sound small limes; place them in a saucepan on the hot range, with one wineglassful of white wine (but not Rhine wine); let reduce to three quarters—which will take about six minutes.  Place a clean napkin over a bowl; pour the whole over the napkin; fold it up at both ends, then sharply twist the ends in different directions, until the juice is all squeezed into the bowl. Have a preparation the same as in No. 91, and use the above instead of the vanilla, proceeding with the rest exactly in the same way.

## 95. *Omelet à la M. Ballou.*

Grind two heaped tablespoonfuls of fresh roasted coffee (Java and Mocha by preference). Pour in a saucepan on the hot range one and a half cups of fresh milk, adding four and a half ounces of powdered sugar, and as soon as the milk boils, immediately add the coffee, thoroughly mixing with a spoon meanwhile; tightly cover the pan and place it on the corner of the range to infuse for three minutes, taking special care not to let it boil again. Strain it through a fine napkin into another saucepan, and let it cool off; add then three tablespoonfuls of *rice flour*, thoroughly beat it with a whip, place it on the fire, and continually stir until it comes to a boil; then place the pan on the corner of the range and let slowly cook for twelve minutes. Make an omelet as in No. 46, and just before folding it up, place half of the preparation right in the centre, fold up, turn it onto a hot silver dish; liberally dredge the omelet with powdered sugar, glaze the surface with a red iron. Slide down a small tube into a pastry-bag, pour the rest of the preparation in, make a fancy border around the omelet, and send it to the table.

## 96. *Eggs-Cocotte.*

Have six small thoroughly cleaned cocotières ready. Chop up, very fine, one medium-sized, sound peeled shallot, and the half of a sound peeled onion; place them in a sautoire on the range with a tablespoonful of butter, and cook slowly for three minutes, taking care not to let get brown. Chop up, very fine, twenty-four canned mushrooms, add them to the rest with one tablespoonful of freshly chopped parsley, and a teaspoonful of chopped chervil (if at hand); season with a tablespoonful of salt and a teaspoonful of pepper, mix all well together with the spatula for a second, then add a gill of Espagnole sauce (No. 105), and let all cook slowly for five minutes.

Pour a tablespoonful of the sauce into each cocotière, then break a fresh egg into each cocotière, pour a teaspoonful of the sauce over each egg, well spread. Place the cocotières on a tin dish, and bake in a very hot oven for two minutes. Remove from out the oven, lay them on a dish with a folded napkin and send to the table.

## 97. *Omelet à la Mrs. W. L. Brown.*

Place in a pan two ounces of chocolate, with just enough milk to dissolve it on the hot range; add a cup and a half of fresh milk; continually stir until it comes to a boil. Dilute two tablespoonfuls of rice flour into two tablespoonfuls of milk, and add it to the chocolate, stirring briskly meanwhile; place the pan on the corner of the range, and let gently simmer for fifteen minutes, but do not allow it to boil.

Have an omelet made as in No. 46, and, before folding, place half of the preparation right in the centre, fold up, turn it over a hot silver dish. Place the balance of the preparation into a pastry-bag, with a small tube previously slided down; and by pressing the preparation, make a nice rosette at each end of the omelet. Decorate the dish all around with six lady-fingers, cut in triangular shaped pieces ; carefully press a little of the contents of the bag on each piece of lady-fingers, so as to have them represent pretty, small roses. Liberally dredge them with powdered sugar, then glaze the omelet with a red iron, and then send to the table.

N. B.—All these sweet omelets should always be promptly made for the time of serving, otherwise it would be sufficient cause to fail to have them to perfection.

## 98. *Eggs-Cocotte à la Wm. Bracken.*

Prepare and proceed exactly the same as No. 96, only substituting one gill of hot Allemande sauce (No. 111) for the gill of Espagnole sauce (No. 105), and serve the same.

## 99. *Fried Eggs for Garnishing.*

Pour half a gill of sweet oil into the frying-pan; when the oil is hot break in one egg. carefully closing up the white part with a skimmer, so as to have it firm, and in a single form. Only one at the time should be cooked, and two minutes will be sufficient.

## 100. *Egg Stuffed à la Higgins.*

Prepare in a sautoire one ounce of good butter, two tablespoonfuls of grated Parmesan cheese, and a tablespoonful of grated Swiss cheese, place the sautoire on the corner of the range, slowly stir with the spatula until dissolved and well mixed. Cut one ounce of smoked beef tongue into very thin julienne shaped pieces, one good sized sound truffle, and four mushrooms cut the same way. Add now half a wine glass of white wine (but not sweet) to the cheese, mix the wine and cheese well together, then add the tongue, truffle, and mushrooms.

Cut six hard shelled boiled eggs in halves lengthwise, remove the yolks without breaking the whites; mash the yolks and place in the pan with the rest of the preparation, mix the whole well together for three minutes while cooking.

Stuff the twelve half whites with the preparation—up to the level; then close them, so as to represent six original eggs. Have a silver dish, lightly buttered, ready, then arrange the balance of the stuffing right in the centre of the dish, giving a pyramid shape; place the eggs at the base of the pyramid upright, so they will lightly lean against it.

Cover the whole with a gill of very thick tomato sauce highly seasoned, sprinkle a very little grated Parmesan cheese over all, then place in the oven for fifteen minutes. Remove from the oven and serve very hot.

# APPENDIX.

## 101. *Bouillon Blanc—white broth.*

Place in a large stock-urn on a moderate fire a good heavy knuckle of a fine white veal with all the débris, or scraps of meat, including bones, remaining in the kitchen (but not of game); cover fully with cold water, adding a handful of salt; and as it comes to a boil, be very careful to skim all the scum off—no particle of scum should be left on—and then put in two large, sound, well-scraped carrots (whole), one whole, cleaned, sound turnip, one whole, peeled, large, sound onion, one well-cleaned parsley root, three thoroughly washed leeks, and a few leaves of cleaned celery. Boil very slowly for six hours on the corner of the range; keenly skim the grease off ; then strain well through a wet cloth into a china bowl or a stone jar, and put it away in a cool place for general use.

## 102. *Croûtons for Soups.*

Cut some dice-shaped pieces of bread, and fry them in a pan with clarified butter; when a rich golden color, drain, and add to the soup when needed.

## 103. *Sauce Demi-Glace, or Madeira.*

Add one small glassful of mushroom liquor to one pint of good Espagnole sauce (No. 105); also a small glassful of Madeira wine, a bouquet (No. 106), and a scant teaspoonful of pepper. Remove the fat carefully and cook for thirty minutes, leaving the sauce in a rather liquid state; then strain and use when needed. This takes the place of all Madeira sauces.

117

### 104. *Batter for Fritters.*

Mix a quarter of a pound of sifted flour in a small basin, with half a pint of lukewarm water, to which three-quarters of an ounce of fresh butter has been added. Place in a saucepan, which should be tilted on the range so that when the water boils the butter can be skimmed off the top. Add, if necessary, a little more water to make a soft paste, beating well with a spatula, to keep it free from lumps, and of a proper consistence; it must be gray and compact-looking. Add just a little warm water to render the paste soft and diluted, although sufficiently thick to cover the objects for which it is intended; that means, it must drop easily from the spoon. Add to this half a pinch of salt and two egg-whites; beat well together for one minute, and use at once.

### 105. *Sauce Espagnole—for one gallon.*

Mix one pint of raw, strong mirepoix (No. 107) with two ounces of good fat (chicken's fat is preferable). Mix with the compound four ounces of flour, and moisten with one gallon of white broth (No. 101). Stir well, and then add, if handy, some baked veal and ham bones. Boil for three hours, and then remove the fat very carefully; rub the sauce through a very fine sieve, and keep it for many purposes in cooking.

### 106. *A Bouquet—how to prepare.*

Take four branches of well-washed parsley-stalks—if the branches be small, take six—one branch of soup-celery, well washed; one blade of bay-leaf, one sprig of thyme, and two cloves, placed in the centre of the parsley, so as to prevent cloves, thyme, and bay-leaf from dropping out of the bouquet while cooking; fold it well, and tightly tie with a string, and use when required in various ways.

118

## 107. *Mirepoix*.

Stew in a saucepan two ounces of fat, two carrots, one onion, one sprig of thyme, one bay-leaf, six whole peppers, three cloves, and, if handy, a ham bone cut into pieces. Add two sprigs of celery and half a bunch of parsley roots; cook for fifteen minutes, and use when directed in other recipes. Scraps of baked veal may also be added, if at hand.

## 108. *Béchamel Sauce*.

Place in a saucepan two ounces of butter, add two tablespoonfuls of flour, and stir constantly for five minutes. Moisten with a pint and a half of boiling milk, being careful to pour it in gradually; then beat it well with a whisk. Add half a teaspoonful of grated nutmeg, a pinch of salt, a bouquet (No. 106), twelve whole peppers, and a little mushroom liquor, if at hand. Cook well for fifteen minutes, and when done rub through a fine sieve.

## 109. *White-Roux*.

Put in a saucepan two ounces of butter, and place it on the corner of the hot range, add to it two tablespoonfuls of flour, keep stirring constantly for seven minutes. Then let it cool, and when cold, use in various sauces as directed.

## 110. *Sauce Périgueux*.

Chop up very fine two fine truffles; place them in a sautoire with a glassful of Madeira wine. Reduce on the hot stove for five minutes. Add half a pint of Espagnole sauce (No. 105). Just allow to come to a boil, and serve very hot.

## 111. *Sauce Allemande.*

Melt two ounces of butter in a saucepan on a slow fire, with three table-spoonfuls of flour to thicken. Stir well, not letting it brown; then moisten with one pint of white broth (No. 101), beating constantly, and cook for ten minutes. Dilute three egg-yolks separately in a bowl. pour the sauce over the eggs, a very little at a time; strain through a Chinese strainer, and finish with half an ounce of good butter and the juice of half a lemon, taking care that it does not boil a second time.

## 112. *Garnishing à la Chipolata—for one gallon.*

Fry a quarter of a pound of salt pork, cut dice-shaped, for two minutes in a saucepan; then add half a pint of carrots cut tubular-shaped, half a pint of onions browned and glazed in the oven (No. 113), one pint of blanched and peeled chestnuts, half a pint of mushrooms, and six small sausages cut in pieces. Add two quarts of Espagnole sauce (No. 105), half a pint of tomato sauce (No. 109), a tablespoonful of salt, and a large teaspoonful of pepper. Cook for thirty minutes, and use when needed.

## 113. *Glazed Onions for Garnishing.*

Select one quart of small onions; peel the sides only, and pare the roots neatly, being careful not to cut them. Place them in a sautoire with half an ounce of clarified butter, and sprinkle them with half a pinch of powdered sugar. Glaze them in a slow oven for fifteen minutes; place them in a stone jar, and use for garnishing when required.

## 114. *Eggs à la Régence.*

Shred an ounce and a half of salt pork into fine pieces (ham will answer the same purpose), also one onion cut into small squares, and six medium-sized mushrooms, all of equal size; moisten with a spoonful of good gravy, and cook for five minutes.

## 115. *Sauce Velouté.*

Melt one ounce of good butter in a saucepan, adding two tablespoonfuls of flour, and stir well, not letting it get brown. Moisten with a pint and a half of good veal and chicken stock, the stronger the better. Throw in a garnished bouquet (No. 106), half a cupful of mushroom liquor, if at hand, six whole peppers, half a pinch of salt, and a very little nutmeg. Boil for twenty minutes, stirring continuously with a wooden spatula; then remove to the side of the fire, skim thoroughly and let it continue simmering slowly for one hour. Then rub through a fine sieve. This sauce will make the foundation for any kind of good white stock.

## 116. *Lobster Butter.*

Extract the coral from one cooked lobster (the eggs may be used instead); pound it in a mortar to a paste, mixing it with one ounce of good butter and a teaspoonful of mustard. Rub through a fine sieve, and keep in a cool place. The butter can also be used for coloring purposes.

## 117. *Purée of Chestnuts.*

Boil one pound of chestnuts for ten minutes; peel and skin them immediately, put them in a saucepan with one quart of white broth (No. 101), a tablespoonful of salt, and two teaspoonfuls of pepper and a quarter of a pound of butter. Let all boil well for thirty minutes; rub through a sieve, and use when needed.

121

### 118. *Sauce à la Poulette.*

Put one pint of hot Allemande sauce (No. 111) into a saucepan, with one ounce of fresh butter; adding the juice of half a medium-sized lemon, and a teaspoonful of chopped parsley. Heat well on the hot stove until thoroughly melted and mixed, but do not let it boil. Keep the sauce warm, and serve for all sauce poulettes.

### 119. *Cream Sauce.*

Take half a pint of béchamel sauce (No. 108); add half an ounce of butter, and beat them together carefully, adding half a cupful of sweet cream. Then serve.

### 120. *Sauce Colbert.*

Put in a saucepan half a pint of very thick Madeira sauce (No. 103); add to it very gradually one ounce of good, fresh butter, also two tablespoonfuls of meat-glaze (No. 121). Mix well together without boiling; then squeeze in the juice of half a sound lemon, and add one teaspoonful of chopped parsley when serving.

### 121. *Meat Glaze.—Glace de Viande.*

As this meat glaze, when properly made, will keep in perfect condition for any length of time, I would advise that half a pint be made at a time, in the following manner: Place in a large saucepan ten quarts of white broth (No. 101), or nine quarts of consommé, and reduce it on a moderate fire for fully four hours, at which time it should be reduced to half a pint. Transfer it in a stone jar or bowl; put a cover on, and keep in a cool place for general use.

www.ingramcontent.com/pod-product-compliance
Lightning Source LLC
Chambersburg PA
CBHW011800040426
42448CB00017B/3319